"*Records Ruin the Landscape* is highly recommended and a must-read for anyone probing new music and recordings." — PETER GENA, *CAA Reviews*

"For compositions whose whole raison d'être is to generate a drastically different realization with every performance . . . no recording of any one performance could be said to 'be' the piece. . . . David Grubbs's exhaustively researched *Records Ruin the Landscape* explores this dilemma specifically as it affected the generation of avant-garde composers who hit their stride in the sixties, John Cage being the most prominent and outspoken among them."
— DAVE MANDL, *Los Angeles Review of Books*

"One of the chief joys of this book is that it seeks to rediscover the avant-gardes of the 1960s in all their spontaneity, in their present-ness, as if unfolding these mavericks from their own perspectives, without benefit of current hindsight. We learn, reading this book, what the future looked like to the past. *Records Ruin the Landscape* seeks to prestidigitate the landscape of the 1960s back to life. For this, one should be thankful — including for the recordings that allow David Grubbs' act of imagination and scholarship to have taken place."
— DANIEL HERWITZ, *Critical Inquiry*

"As a whole, it is the dialogic aspect of *Records Ruin the Landscape* that marks it as a necessary read for scholars, artists, and listeners across artistic and academic disciplines. Through an endlessly alluring rhetorical style combined with vast stores of primary source material, Grubbs offers new insights on old questions from a variety of perspectives, placing previously disparate discourses into productive conversation." — MIKE D'ERRICO, *Popular Music and Society*

NOW THAT THE AUDIENCE IS ASSEMBLED

—howev

of two opposing breaths of two opposing breaths

small, however quiet

o

no longer listening

The wave crashed
With breath following breath,

instrument

The curl ripped
with breath hocketing breath
, airily unvoiced

Now that the audience is assembled

David Grubbs

DUKE UNIVERSITY PRESS   DURHAM AND LONDON   2018

© 2018 DUKE UNIVERSITY PRESS
Printed in the United States of America on acid-free paper ∞
Designed by Matthew Tauch
Typeset in Garamond Premier Pro by Tseng Information
Systems, Inc.

Library of Congress Cataloging-in-Publication Data
Names: Grubbs, David, [date] author.
Title: Now that the audience is assembled / David Grubbs.
Description: Durham : Duke University Press, 2018. |
Includes bibliographical references and index.
Identifiers: LCCN 2017045251 (print) | LCCN 2017051026
(ebook)
ISBN 9780822371588 (ebook)
ISBN 9780822371380 (hardcover : alk. paper)
ISBN 9780822371472 (pbk. : alk. paper)
Subjects: LCSH: Music—Performance—Poetry. | Improvisation
(Music)—Poetry. | Avant-garde (Music) | Music in literature.
Classification: LCC PS3557.R76 (ebook) | LCC PS3557.R76 N69
2018 (print) | DDC 811/.54—dc23
LC record available at https://lccn.loc.gov/2017045251

Cover Art: John Sparagana, *Untitled*, 2017, inkjet prints sliced
and mixed on paper. Courtesy of Corbett vs. Dempsey. Photos:
Aron Gent.

Contents

Now that the audience is assembled for the musician's

bruited first contact with an instrument we can't yet visualize and

cannot imagine what it could be made to sound like

The figure slowly makes as if to remove an instrument from a case whose contours remain obscure. For all we know the case has always been leaning in the corner of this darkened, already stage-lit room. Always behind the door that just closed itself. Or was closed by a swift, unnoticed hand. There was a door ajar upstage center and then it was closed and the room sealed.

When's our start time?

The instrument waits in a case that's free of the first sign of wear. For all we can see it looks as if it has never left this room. The room itself is newly painted—a blackened gray-blue, a color to absorb sound—and free of dust. It looks as if it has never left, never been left, never been anywhere but behind the door.

The audience conducts last-minute stretching exercises in their seats.

Regarding the concealed instrument's design it would be inadvisable to say anything other than nightfall in the covered cage. Nor is it possible to hazard whether the instrument is in tune, if it will function as it should, even the extent to which it can be made to cooperate. How should it function? Not now. What's the occasion to rise as if there had been no waiting, a hush, a wave

rushing the length of the room silences exchanges, catchings-up,

now time's upon us. Do you recognize the figure

The gangly silhouette crossing the stage area—the lighted rectangle without chairs, without audience, its rear two corners touching the back wall of this circular room—might be this evening's wrangler, a stagehand or tech person qualified to decide whether what's in the case formerly behind the door is ready to function as an instrument. Is ready to rodeo. There are degrees of cooperation, and we've all seen instruments that refuse to cooperate and are no less the instrument for it. Are ready or not to play nice. Perhaps they're less desirable from the perspective of the performer, or less desirable from the vantage of the audience, but there will be no angry tearing off of stripes, no shaming, no expulsion from tonight's event. The tickets have been time-stamped, everyone clocked in

the audience is upon us, time's gathered

when stepping fully out of shadow the figure becomes recognizable as tonight's performer, a musician inclined toward for lack of a better term improvising, accepting, making do, jerry-rigging, thinking on her feet, famously hashing it out in public; real-time instrument invention, construction, demolition, repair, and referral; solo repurposing, duo repurposing, trio and large-ensemble, not to give too much away but tonight solo and in first contact with and maybe one-time contact with the waiting instrument.

How could it be made to sound

unrecognizable instrument

laid bare in the musician's x-ray gaze, that supersensory sometime dividing line between performer and audience, upstage where there had been a door and where now there's just door erased and sketched-in, blue-gray, blackened space? Space of audience and performer — solo performer, real-time and shared-time instrument builder — and of the brightly lit rectangle of stage abutting these listless, stretching bodies. Every seat is occupied. If the instrument is unrecognizable, how should it be assembled? Downbeat. What sounds occur in the process of preparing the instrument we can't picture and can't picture sounding? Gambit. What's shared time?

Picture breath striking solid.

Picture breath and mineral, brilliantly polished mineral. Breath-polished mineral. Picture breath and unbreakable retrofuturist compound. Picture breath unopposed, breath unceasing, breath and flesh and the audience softly inhales. With breath traversing aperture, with breath funneled through aperture, with breath so vigorously tunneling. The audience exhales, all those sated lungs. The audience breathes in a bit closer to unison, and we still have time — shard time, scads of — to act as one, it will be done.

Picture the instrument in no one's memory. Picture the instrument yet to be summoned. Picture the instrument the musician hasn't in fact held or beheld, the instrument the musician's far from assembling. Picture breath stopped short. With breath artfully diverted. With breath whistling across aperture in the dark.

A longer rest, a slower rest

A merciless combining of shorter rests

A downshift and a density change

The musician breathes in and the audience breathes out, a mid-air meeting. The faintest overture of aerial skirmishes. The musician exhales, with breath striking cord. With breath exciting cord. With breath zinging the length of fleshy cord, with breath exciting increasingly shorter divisions. To sing. With breath to sing these progressively smaller lengths of cord doing their damnedest, voiceprint and thumbprint, to color, to jab, and to smear, to cast one's lot and one's ballot, to find and satisfyingly hold aloft

a pitch, a purple thumb present and accounted for upon the memory surface of audience. Breath and sounding body now without stopping, now without separating one gesture from another, held and ongoing

and so an unheard next.

Without repeating

Without recognizing repetition as such

Without believing repetition

Now it's the audience's turn. It exhales still more convincingly with a single breath. The musician inhales, bends her steps upstage toward the door erased. Feedback is the consequence of listeners' intensity of focus. A musician occasionally may fool an instrument and an amplifier into believing that he or she represents the will of the audience, acts as a delegate. The musician breathes in and sounds the deciding vote.

Time's upon us all with eyes

on the lighted rectangle. With breath guarded, with breath surrendered. With flutelike reanimated voice, with holographic unsteadiness, with swagger and flicker. With a satisfyingly husky stripe of feedback, to sing, delivered at the volume of a reassuring speaking voice, to some so reassuring a voice as to trouble. With breath and body sundered, the stuttered vowel resolves itself into an *o* captured and stretched like *so*, a human *o* in red laser.

A dogged worrying of a modest patch of ground

the quietest feedback

scaled to the volume of flutelike voice

Feedback swims aboveground.

Feedback swims about our heads. Feedback swims in mid-air, by its nature seeks to exhaust itself, fails. Feints, fails, falls forward, falls end over end. Pratfalls downbeatlessly. Flails. It's a nervous habit of occasionally gorgeous footprinting, an animal shifting of weight from hoof to paw to hand, infinity catching tail.

So give it back. Share alike this unamplified *o*, unending vowel, our holographic feedback. Feedback sustains, is nothing but interior, audience and musician alike enclosed no matter how quiet.

A rip curl closes. A ribbed sphere, a magnetically charged interior. Feedback impresses not as object but as location, even this *o*. Unprepossessing feedback. *So.*

The sine wave can always be counted on to thread the needle. Deathlessly penetrate the immobilized eye. How can the audience inhabit so modest a sound? Indifferent feedback, where there had been a door. Sound to envelop a lighted rectangle and more. A diagnostic red laser touches retina, radically expands. So quiet inside this *o* and yet upon us it seizes breath. It holds breath. Without separating one gesture from another, without repeating, without recognizing, without acknowledging repetition as such, without believing, and without to anyone's satisfaction describing, it clicks off.

Red aural afterimage.

With breath held, I could have you expelled.

En-

counterpoint

of two opposing breaths. In the absence of feedback, however quiet, the audience resumes the exercise of breathing as one. One breath for now after the last and after the next. A hush, a wave, a sequence, a series, and

0

no longer listening within a sound. Within an interior now voided. Within an interior now forgotten. The wave crashed. The curl ripped. The rip had it, had had having had it. With breath following breath, with breath hocketing breath, audience and musician encounter one another as airily unvoiced instruments.

Two breaths vectored

Two breaths insensate

Two breaths just sliding past

Two breaths shaped and detached

Two breaths set on glide, the both unaware

Two breaths exiting opposite, and neither moves the other

merely cords and their divisions, stacking and balancing multiples on multiples within multiples. Crossing divisions. No breath stilling cord, no cord stilling breath. The fill before the expand before the just sliding by. No breath stills another. Hexed human cords sensing, blackly picturing, shaping each breath — hexed cords coordinated just *o* — and the mirrored breaths rushing past one by one to disappear soundless stage right and left.

Broken specters long since fled.

No breath and no memory, let's do it again.

To produce no sound and to provoke none.

The mystery of what's inside the case climaxes with the musician's comic theatrical stumble and sudden unnecessary dusting (an exclamatory exhale, breath striking solid with no visible result) and perfunctory sleeve-polishing, a skeleton key fingernail inserted with a brief, suspenseful wriggle in its oversized lock, four clicks of the latches, and it's a brief matter of time upon us breathes the audience.

Then an awful clattering shake

and

spills forth

disassembled, manifold

truly unrecognizable as instrument

a dirty heap dominating the stage dumped inconclusively out.

The musician considers the spill that covers the stage. She looks every bit as surprised as the audience, every bit as disappointed.

Audience, musician, heap.

The performance begins or begins again with the selection, inspection, and sounding of parts. The categorizing and the sorting of parts. The task of sounding parts individually, parts representing any number of potential instruments to emerge from, to be assembled from cast-off elements slumbering within the pile. For some in the audience the process begins with the least urgency, the least physical effort, and not without provocation.

In the absence of mind's-eye touch

In the absence of mind's-eye breath striking

In the absence of scale, degree, even of continuum

The performance initially impresses as little more than pauses, hesitant touches, and nearly soundless breaths.

The musician walks lightly atop the heap of parts, lest it should shift and she damage the instrument or herself be injured. She steps cautiously and comes to a halt only with exquisite care. The audience attunes to landslide, cratering, potential onstage avalanche. With a tenuous footing she bends down to select from this filthy, rusted glacier a promising pebble covered in ice-blue cellophane. Before the marveling audience she unwraps a piece of whitish translucent candy and pops it into her mouth.

One part vanished, just like that. The musician dispenses with the hard candy in several loud bites. The heap appears to all eyes undiminished. The musician paces, and the audience stiffens. The musician bends at the waist, shakes her head, and resumes her slow steps, sifting through the rubble with her feet, from time to time squatting or kneeling down to gather a handful of detritus. To select, to sift, to let fall, and occasionally to sound the individual piece whether by striking, squeezing, blowing, rubbing, chewing, or swallowing. Footsteps through the snowdrift in self-interrupting sequence.

A slow march.

A frozen march, an icebreaker.

Surely the instrument need not be so complex. Of how many pieces should it be composed? Nothing requires it to be so artfully scavenged a thing. The musician's criteria remain obscure, are glimpsed only intermittently through abrupt assemblages and sculptural false starts. She sounds the search for the right handful. This is a solo performance; how labor-intensive an instrument can one individual execute in the time that's upon us? Bowerbird amid the spill. To assemble to her satisfaction, however irrelevant that word. The audience sinks deeper into its seats. We may be hard to read out here in the darkness, but we're not without concern.

The effect of the audience on the tempo of unfolding

on scale, given the tempo of this

our exhale

The musician's pacing gradually begins to reshape the heap, to sculpt with her feet the starting gun's spill, the rusted fishes and loaves.

Once there was a door and simpler times before the performance began. Now the instrument's case lies within the heap. The musician continues to truffle wrapped candies, absently popping trompe l'oeil chunks from a tetanus-blooming glacier.

Patient, distracted steps, and her at times calf-, knee-, or waist-deep wading reorganize the pile into a series of ridges and paths. One can foresee the performer sinking herself into a system of canals, locks, lunar lanes.

Of shoulder-height sheer faces

of paths between piles:

landscape

The audience surges. It leans forward as one and completes the circuit of shoulders brushing shoulders, electron leaps, of shared commitment and empathy. Hard-won mutabilities for alien criteria. For the devising of tonight's great icy Kentucky and its on-the-fly Canal Street, Division Street, Washington, Jefferson, Market, Walnut, Chestnut, MLK, Malcolm X, and Muhammad Ali Boulevard. For spectators intending intensification of focus, briefed or breved in the perception of such and the suspension of touch, shoulder to electroquavering shoulder.

Send it down the line

and here it comes again, echoing at you and sweeping past. Greetings to your neighbor, a miniscule leap, and no one needs to understand the math. Intending a wave, intending an arc, revisiting points along a circuit.

The most helpful member of the audience suddenly locks onto the presence of a partially disinterred music stand. He springs from his seat to dig and to separate stand from heap, and in the process alters in countless ways the instrument in the making. After the music stand is placed just so, a flag marking the Iwo Jima of his precise specifications, he turns to the musician and impatiently gestures with, for all to see, three taps on an imaginary wristwatch:

Shall we start? Don't tell me that we began who knows when. Don't snow me, and don't snow us all with explanations of performance immemorial and the intermittence of listening. (An accelerated pantomime of a snore and jerking awake.) Time was when? Upon whom? The musician gapes, blinks. The helpful audience member positions himself down lighted rectangle left beside one of the heap's more impressive canals, and to the surprise of all present he indicates with a cocksure hitchhiker's thumb a scavenged, worse-for-wear copy of a score.

This should solve any questions that might arise.

The volunteer from the audience has done his best to smooth out the crumpled score, to make it readable to the musician and presentable to the audience. He stands knee-deep in trash, eager to assume page-turning duties. Three more taps, this time upon the stained front cover of the score. Are we ready? He flashes a lottery-winner smile to the audience, allows it to evaporate just as quickly, and pivots back to the musician with a mask of determination. The two figures symmetrically lean in toward the score and share a squint. The audience purrs.

We drink up the duo's silent, synchronized eye movements and their careful parsing of the ragged score. Two audience members in the back row take this opportunity to turn, lock eyes, and gently touch long-stemmed glasses of red wine — a toast to one another. A flash goes off to commemorate the alliance of musician and page-turner, and the photographer is set upon by a small mob of neighboring audience members who quietly and devastatingly reprimand him with eyebrows and glares. No more photography. No more interruptions. When the two figures onstage complete their businesslike reading of the score — mutual nods, snaps of the neck — the page-turner visibly relaxes.

Reset for the counting in.

A meaningful pause at

zero time

and

with two hands

interlocked and eight fingers interlaced and ramping up to the maximum pressure that she can exert in an attempt to pulverize between hard, dry palms another rusted treasure from the heap, the musician neglects to the clear disappointment of the helpful audience member the first and most basic instruction in the score:

Compose a gesture that can be repeated.

Ignoring this, and sidestepping any meaningful assertion of physical mastery she rubs, scrapes, blows on, whistles across, endeavors to crush, with crossed eyes balances on the bridge of her nose, and shakes violently for a disturbingly long spell various small implements before slashing a monitory calligraphic xXx into the wall, all part of a series of actions through which the audience recognizes a performer unwilling to repeat herself.

No improvising

coughs the page-turner, and his frustration and perplexity ripple through the audience. The score is clear on this point: begin with a gesture. Just one. Prepare a single gesture that can be repeated. Compose yourself. You needn't start by fishing for the novel implement nor anticipating the rarest of discoveries from the heap. You needn't start with the disassemblage, and the universe of this piece of music doesn't begin with the big spill. Zero time means start time. Not prior to the beginning, and not with the most preliminary searching and sifting. No hashing it out in public, no so-called real-time research. Count us in, but never in the absence of an instrument. Don't start with the hope that an instrument will suggest itself. Don't imagine one emerging from the mud, being harvested from the glacier, sourced and with spellbinding pathos conceived and crafted in our presence on an overnight watch recapitulating the timeline of evolution from primordial sea to lighted rectangle. Where do you see that in the score?

I'm turning the page now.

The pitcher atop the mound of refuse shakes it off. Stubbornly brushes off signal after signal from the page-turner. A gesture, he says again, capable of being repeated. One in a recognizable series — at which point we might begin to consider it a musical gesture.

The lighted rectangle remains a sodden spill of biblical volume, a vast multiplication outward from a point now merely rumored. One can view the heap itself as a single instrument, and one can foresee a nearly limitless number of instruments to be excavated and fashioned from the landscape. Score and page-turner be damned, the musician remains intent on prospecting, on sifting, sorting, and sounding one piece at a time, on publicly auditioning unique fragments.

Repetition as such.

Be certain that the repetition passes for exact.

The musician defaults to no expression, resumes her work. Faces away from the page-turner. Appears intensely interested in something that looks like a shattered, weaponized fragment of a videocassette. Wipes it on her sleeve, spit shines, and carefully places it in a back pocket.

The page-turner ignores this and similar affronts.

Do your homework, thrice fingerpoints the page-turner. Don't start improvising the very means of sound production when the score clearly demands an integral instrument. Arrive prepared and ready to play. It's implied by the fact of the score, no matter — holding the rank, deteriorating object at arm's length — its condition. Is it the place of the score to stipulate that you know your instrument? Know where the instrument begins and ends; know cleaning, maintenance, and long-term care; know what's not-instrument; know the instrument's capabilities of producing sound, of rounding off and bringing a gesture to a close; know how to fashion what's replicable.

Know it before the first audience member arrives.

Know history, know Shaker carpentry.

How difficult it must be for the page-turner to ignore the disarticulated heap of pebbles, stones, dirt, mud, menthol candy, Neolithic leather, divination tools, cassette tape, 8-track tape, Beta and VHS, shattered 78 rpm records, antiquated soda bottles, extinct currencies, magazines and newspapers rivaling the half-century accumulation in your grandparents' basement, ladies' shoes, men's shoes, kids' and babies' shoes, spiderwebbed windshields, quivers of wipers, cases of fluids, all manner of industrial lubricants, the barest husk of a Buick ballasted and bottoming out with a trunk full of car batteries — everything short of the sound of electric blues coming at you several decades of Sundays ago on Maxwell Street.

Dig

and you may find more conventionally musical strata: a vein of beginner-sized violins, bridges, bows, paper envelopes with coils of steel string, plastic recorders, school-band instruments in destroyed unbreakable cases, odd fragments of Califone record players, stacks of hymnals, a grand piano's harp, and various demolished frames and skeletons and coordinating structures. All that remains is to choose.

Magnetic pathway

holes await your breath

a volume of air so easily disturbed

How long has it been since the first seat was filled, how long since the performance began, how long walking blues and how long dissembling blues, how long since breath and breath skirmished and exited opposite, how long since the audience first exhaled as one, how long since beginning the quietly sounded labor of assembling the cast-off parts, how long since musician and page-turner first faced off?

Reset for the counting down.

We're ready, we're asleep already.

Another shard secreted. Squirreled in a pocket.

Defiance.

Toss it unsorted, pitch it unfiled, reshuffle in abeyance of style. Multiplication of flowering phyla among the paths and piles of gray- and black-streaked volcanic landscape.

Upon which the lighted

rectangle, the visible boundary, within which

the patient inspection of what might count as sounding a repeat

It dawns on the more wakeful half of the audience that each piece re-trieved from the heap skews smaller than the previous. A fatalistic cast is felt: we tend in the direction of dust.

Sound the assembling and hopefully in the not-so-distant sound the final assemblage of siftings. The other half of the audience descends to the edge of sleep. To sound or not sound, to stir or allow to settle, to gradually narcotize. The musician fashions a performance of delays or, according to the page-turner, games the audience by delaying the start of the performance with ever-lengthening intervals, with tangled-up rests and syrupy downshifts in adroit time-scale counterpoise to the less and less substantial objects summoned from the pile.

To winnow from pebble to powder to what hangs in the air.

The individual implement as atmospheric fleck

as matter in particulate form, as inhalant. The half of the audience that's starkly awake has not acclimated to this room, has not been able to find a comfortable position. They experiment with sitting upright, with sliding down plank-style to facilitate straightened spines, or with heads hanging lapward, lanternlike. Palms mop brows and fingers un-comb hair. They're especially agitated by the lengthening swells of slower unison breathing from the part of the audience that has shaded sleepwise. They're distressed, still wondering whether the performance has begun—helpless exchanges of looks with the page-turner, one of their own—distressed over whether the component parts gleaned, sounded, and classified by the musician are in fact sifting smaller, dis-tressed at where this tends and where this may not end. At where it does not begin. Distressed by the endless chaining of rests, nautilus movement.

Insomniac ascent

or death-cult decrescendo

that's the choice as understood by the half of the audience resentful of its counterpart's downward displacement into sleep. A twitchy soul darts forward and plucks from the heap in staccato succession a dozen wrapped candies and distributes them to the restless occupants of the first several rows.

Those smallest sounds of onstage discovery are suddenly and decisively rendered indiscernible against a rising, unfamiliar noise floor of metal grinding against metal. Squalling machinic friction caroms upward from well underground, the space of the performance evidently sited and balanced directly above the uptown express rounding the slowest, most torturous bend, the number five train making a sweep across the low-frequency band during a time of precious little onstage activity. Face to face it makes your eyes rattle. Here, this many stories above, feet and knees sense the distant climax.

How many stories down to the underground? Subway reveries take hold. In smaller towns people dream the existence of improbable and unnecessary subways. Traveling city-folk dream about the subway even when abroad and attempting to forgive or back-burner the city.

See if we see you in your dreams.

See if we see you in our dreams, intones the half of us asleep already.

Listen to the wind outside.

Strange that in this sealed-off, windowless bunker we can hear any trace of what's beyond, but the wind has risen and choruses. For ears attuned to any input, audible gustings mask the onstage sounds.

The wind emboldens a beery soul who can't take it any longer. He jumps up and stomps the length of a row of seats in an exaggerated pantomime of the musician. Mocking footfalls in fictive zero-gravity boots and fake truffling into and out of the pockets of neighboring audience members earn him a mixture of laughter and scorn. Others similarly threaten to stand up and scatter the cards, wind authorizing.

A second figure jumps to his feet, but instead of joining the insurrection takes long, rapid strides toward the protestor and surprises him from behind with a kick in the ass.

It's an extraordinary sound.

The wind ramps up, swirls, and all present and awake brace for the confrontational spinning around, the fists or full-body grappling, and the consequent choosing of sides. The drunk comedian unexpectedly steps out of his imaginary weighted boots, reverses course, and apologizes repeatedly while making his way back down the row. He reseats himself, slumps, and violent winds lull him to sleep.

Once the commotion has dissipated, the performer signals that she has completed her research and is ready to assemble the instrument.

Two shades of melismatic snore color the room.

Push-pull, see-saw.

The musician unearths a picnic-table bench with the roughness and apparent age of a plank from a log cabin.

She uses it to lay out a row of objects from what we now understand as the keep pile. No longer hidden between cupped palms nor stowed in back pockets, the instrument ultimately extends to six feet in length. Several spotlights make the snakelike array of implements glow, and dust positively jives in shafts of light.

Mud joins crinoid fossil to stoneware, to earthenware, to rubber tubing, to pipette, to syringe, and finally to speaker cone as the musician patiently secures each joint, slipping her fingers beneath the body of the instrument to test the solidity of the sequence, to consider the collection as one thing.

Senecan sentences the less complex construction chiefly

running style unspool a single line of

acceleration.

As the instrument grows, the pile shrinks and large swaths of stage are recovered. Avenues widen, and once-sheer, vertiginous faces are reduced to rubble. The retreat of the glacier reveals the instrument's case — the origin of this world's controlled spill and burn — without a scuff.

You'll remember a time or

dream of lightning-strike interjections meshing sound and image. Sound to picture and picture to sound, twilit and afterimaged in the clangor of the uptown express.

Some in the audience dream branching consequences: a dispiriting narrative in which a broken, chastised soloist gives up and decides to disassemble the instrument before it's completed. Addressing the insomniac audience the musician gingerly lifts and horizontally balances the precarious, implausible column of primitive horn, and to mute rapture tilts skyward this hypothesized earliest instrument. She excites fleshy cord, presses aperture to lowermost aperture — the opposite end of the instrument jabs at the ceiling — and applies the minimum possible force of breath to generate this flut-

trr

There you have it. Revel in the unfamiliar trilling hum, its balm and solace. The end of the demonstration coincides with a room-wide final post-orgasm exhale, one forever impressed upon the sleeping portion of audience.

trr

.

to

.

ooo

to

to which

to whom, now

.

three distinct knocks

three from within the unblemished case

the page-turner, stagehand, now the props manager

rushes to help and perhaps it will be faster to remove the hinges

.

This second mystery of the case similarly climaxes with a comic theatrical stumble — the page-turner's overeager, unamusing one — followed by his brandishing of a horrific riposte of a shiv conveniently strong enough to pry loose the hinges of the box. It spills forth a brushed-wool suit pulsing with gray and white soft-focus sine waves, a pair of flower-patterned combat boots, and a diminutive older gentleman

clutching a pristine copy of the score, blinking in the dazzling gloom:

the composer.

The newest arrival gestures toward the instrument and speaks in a novel tongue that after a brief session of trial and error after error it's apparent only the page-turner understands.

By means of this monopolistic relay the composer asks the musician to produce a sound that can be repeated easily, such that over the course of an undetermined number of repetitions it may gradually be transformed. She bends over the picnic-table bench, taking in his words as she reviews the component parts of her instrument. The composer asks the musician to demonstrate what she has prepared.

We understand the musical gesture that follows first and foremost as the performance of symmetry.

The demonstration lasts some number of minutes. Were one to poll the audience, it would likely ballpark the time of the gesture's unfolding, together with its symmetrical refolding, as lasting no less than seven and no more than ten minutes.

The musician's gesture involves the palindromic assembling and dis-assembling of the instrument. She begins by checking the solidity of its many contact points, the rudimentary — mud, straw, and similar — coordination among these mismatched parts. Hollow piece is jammed firmly into hollow piece, bone into bone into stone; joints are pre-pared such that no air can escape; and in a game-changing move con-tact mics are flourished and attached to the instrument by means of a black gummy substance. A half dozen of these small microphones are spread evenly along the felled column, and as she raises the line level and a sixty-cycle ground hum reassures, here again we hold our breaths and witness the musician's precarious task of lifting the in-strument and making sure that it doesn't shatter against the ceiling. With a stoic demeanor and three different hammer-like implements she strikes three different points on the body of the instrument. Three utterly distinct tones resound.

All present, dreaming and otherwise, can't believe what they've heard.

Three bell-like burstings into bloom

followed by their negative image in sound. The third and final tone fades to the satisfaction — this time that is the word — of the audience and before the widened eyes of the composer. Surely the period of real-time, public research has been redeemed, not to speak of everything that went into these three lovely percussive strikes. How does one instrument yield three such perfectly different soundings? How had she known the precise location of each sonorous node? Time spent waiting as denominator, a quick sequence of tones the numerator.

The proportion proves sound; the proportion rings true.

To cross the equator in both directions.

Line level lowered, the sixty-cycle hum evaporates. The contact mics are slowly removed, the black adhesive scraped off, and the cables duly and ably coiled. The instrument is laid horizontal on the bench, and the connections between component parts gently loosened. The instrument returns to the state in which it was found at the onset of the gesture, finds itself once again at the ready:

backward from homestretch into starting gate.

The composer breaches the silence by speaking through the page-turner: I didn't understand. I was listening for a single gesture.

As if animated by magnetic repulsion, the instrument rolls off the bench and crashes to the ground, and the concussive, splintering attack makes everyone jump. Fractured pieces scatter across the floor, roll beneath seats. The musician alone betrays no sign of noticing — no acknowledgement, no emotion — as sleepers rearrange themselves and the light snoring resumes.

Maybe, begins the composer, we need to ask the audience to step outside. This is neither the time nor the place for a public discussion. If a gesture can't be made a second and then a third time, and so on, how will you be able to render plasticity? I was not informed that this would be an open rehearsal.

I need to sense beginning, middle, and end.

It's not necessary that I be able to hold the gesture in mind. I don't need to be able to think it or to silently review it; I need to hear it as one of a series of repetitions. I need for you as the musician to explore the gesture through performing it repeatedly. I will say that it's a pleasure, albeit of a different sort, to examine in my mind the shape of your marvelous solo performance just now, with its three unexpected tones—fortuitous events that I don't imagine I'll encounter again. (The composer scoops up a handful of pieces from the broken instrument and archives them in a back pocket.) The uniqueness of these events colors my experience, and I thank you. (Applause breaks out, abruptly ceases.) When you produce a replicable gesture you are the playback device. You think tape recorder, or perhaps you perform tape recorder. Either way it's much the same. You play back the gesture, and you transform it as you wish or as you deem necessary. Within the world of this composition it really is your decision—I'm just the composer. You transform the sound, thinking the sound or not, holding it in mind or not, inhabiting the metaphor of machine as you prefer, all the while encountering the continuously changing gestures of your fellow performers.

Where are the other performers?

At the same time that the composer addresses his remarks to the performer, a sleeper in the furthest row stirs violently, spasms, and shouts **NO**. She rises with eyes closed and makes her way toward the stage area alternately squeezing between seats and slithering across shoulders. Dreamers and insomniacs clear a path. Mid-pilgrimage she halts and takes the time to recompose by smoothing out her wrinkled dress and extending herself to full height. With an emptied visage she turns to the trio of composer, musician, and page-turner, loudly clears her throat an uncomfortable number of times, and barks in an overloud monotone

YOU   WANT   US   TO   *INTERRUPT*

Oblivious to those parting the sea of seats for her, she resumes her sleepwalk toward the lighted rectangle. Arriving at the edge of the stage she drops to her knees and subject to a rapidly intensifying possession furiously digs at the pile.

Is this another performer? Are there others yet to arrive?

The sleepwalker settles on a single unearthed implement: a box of chalk. Sticking a piece between her lips, she pantomimes flicking a Zippo lighter into flaming gear across her thigh and jams the box deep in the pocket above her heart.

Following the most prominent diagonal canal from downstage right to upstage center, the sleepwalker alters her mien and no longer acknowledges composer, musician, or page-turner. She delivers three urgent raps with her fist on the blue-gray back wall and, to the amazement of all, three knocks echo in response.

The overnight staff listens beyond the door erased. They still haunt this shade.

At their three-knock reply, the sleepwalker presses palms and outstretched fingers hard against the back wall, and with a sustained and room-filling frictive squeal sidesteps her way from the center to extreme upstage right. She squeaks the curved wall as if it were a balloon, and a similar but louder noise is heard with a slight delay as the group on the other side of the wall mirrors her gesture.

The composer's discourse to the musician has reached a stopping point, and they turn as one, turn as does the entire audience, and everyone holds their breath for the duration of the sleepwalker's act of inscribing in chalk on the back wall in four-foot-tall letters:

I

Ranks of sleepers convulse, approach the spike in snoring that precedes eyelids popping open.

HATE

Does anyone really want to see this? The page-turner makes to squelch the interruption but composer and musician simultaneously restrain him, the both grasping an upper arm and gesturing with an index finger laid upon closed lips, eyes silently imploring that he not disrupt the incoming message.

THIS

Fading insomniacs threaten to be pulled beneath, to change places with the now-stirring sleepers, and for an unhurried interval the entire audience indulges in a soulful, deck-clearing yawn.

ROOM

Chalk drop.

The door erased flies open, and six beckoning arms reach out to celebrate, to usher to the other side the sleepwalker. Out cold to the very end, she trips across the threshold and disappears from view as the door soundlessly slams shut.

I redirect your attention to the score.

But first may I see your instrument? The musician gestures at the scatter, and composer and page-turner kneel down and with hands and forearms sweep the debris into a small pyramid at center stage.

Seeking to reengage and reenergize the noticeably less interested musician, the composer hastily twists assemblages of rubble and hands her various miniature reconfigurations of the shattered instrument. Try this. Or this one, which you might be able make sound in the following manner. The composer is himself capable of precise repetitions of improvised figures on nearly any instrument, of transformations both fiendishly incremental — of almost unrecognizably small degrees — and rendered with uncommon patience. In his demonstration of repetition after near repetition he charts an ingenious course such that after a dozen iterations the gesture has been transformed to where most listeners could not identify even a remnant of the original. A musical phrase bolts for the shadows, bends obscure, goes werewolf before watchful eyes.

It disappears into and emerges

from; disappears into

and emerges

from

:

inert

singing glacier

becomes widening river

devolves into thickest graphite trace.

The dark glacier mirror, up-river and down.

Now there are two performers, skating. Composer and musician have settled accounts and set into motion discrete, manipulable gestures. The dry-run duet. Through repeated encounters one phrase imprints itself upon another in this weirdly polite demolition on ice. The audience leans in to track inflections and entanglements. A blind spot whistles my name. Both parties emerge altered from each skirmish declared or not, each slackening of the gravitational field like *so*

and with every near-miss the odds further incline toward fillings loosened.

Cresting a hundredth iteration the two performers modify their inputs to pool resources, to hall of mirrors, and ultimately to generate a dense and tremendously loud column of sound. This inhabitable roar builds upon aural reflections and orients each listener differently. It stacks waxings within wanings within waxings, and comes to define the room. The sound evolves a funnel. It invites surrender, encourages reflections on permanence, and with sober authority summons and offers shelter. After an uncertain period of stasis the audience members gradually allow themselves to recognize a subtle, progressive diminishment within the din, believing that it

loses faith, gains feeling

it really depends on whom you ask. Loses velocity, loses altitude. The duo's composite sound slips below its orbit and enters into a distant, extinguishing plummet as the audience is emboldened to explore the outfield and the lengthening shadow of wall.

The demonstration is scarcely completed when the composer places his instrument on the ground and turns to address the audience.

The musician cannot flip the switch quite so easily, and she rocks back and forth with an unprotesting expression, still cradling her instrument and inhabiting a different sphere while the composer, speaking through the page-turner, shares his take on this brief performance: It needs to be said that a duo performance is something other than this composition. Two is an insufficient number. Two performers suffice only to show the technique. The structure of the work is the invitation for multiple individuals to create and experience alterations on the basis of unforeseen encounters. It's a pleasure to encounter you in this way (composer and page-turner both gesture toward the musician, who gives no indication that she's listening) and to do so again and again and differently each time, but a duo performance has a melancholic desert-island quality. That of two survivors, and we need others. Composer and page-turner toe the edge of the lighted rectangle and peer into the darkness: Do we have volunteers?

The audience feigns sleep or slumbers on.

Thankfully the composer knows when to drop the direct address, and the offer is not repeated. There is no need to force participation. He gestures for musician and page-turner to follow him as he shuffles toward the upstage door that once again swings open. They disappear for several minutes into the unknown region.

When they return to the performance space, they come provisioned with a collection of ten bulky round objects, each thick with dust and wrapped in a maroon cloth and tied with a piece of canary-yellow nylon rope. They lean the wrapped objects against the wall in an arrangement based on descending order of size. The largest of the bundles matches the arm span of the page-turner; the smallest resembles a hubcap.

We're going to try something different, announces the composer.

We're going to work with gongs.

At the magic word the entire audience awakes and frantically begins to make ready. Each person stands up and without a word of instruction folds his or her seat and passes it back to the rear of the room, where they are stacked in neat rows. Everyone is astir. The occupants of the first several rows invade the stage area and with impressive co-ordination shovel and sift what remains of the pile, quickly unearthing a cache of hammers and mallets, a coil of rope, several saw horses, a small butane torch, and a ten-foot pole. A number of working groups organize themselves, beginning with an informal carpenters' guild that proposes to design and construct the structure from which to hang the gongs. Audience members introduce themselves to one another, remark on common acquaintances, and share observations about the evening's progress.

One cadre notable for including the oldest and the youngest members of the audience—brother and sister twins approximately age ten—have volunteered to be musical performers. This most heterogeneous and most enthusiastic of groups kicks into gear with an elaborate warmup of sit-ups, jumping jacks, and stretching exercises.

Another group assists the composer, musician, and page-turner with unwrapping the gongs. The composer launches into a tutorial on the subject of tuning the instruments, beginning with the largest member of the family. All of the gongs will be tuned in reference to its fundamental pitch. With the largest gong suspended on a rope held by two members of the group, the composer sounds the metal by running his hand around the edge of the rim, wetting third and fourth fingers with saliva and making the instrument vibrate ever so slightly with the friction of his touch. He uses the softest mallet available to strike the gong in the center of its nipple-like boss and explores its vibrations by scanning with his left ear an inch above the surface of the instrument.

There's a shimmering both audible and visible

correlated to multiple simultaneous oscillations that over time cede to a fundamental pitch. In tuning the largest gong, the composer alternates between gently striking it dead center with the mallet and raining staccato hammer blows in a circle around the boss. The repetitive, stunted music of tuning — a preparatory music — bends space toward source.

A dissident group favors melting down the gongs and starting again.

They would prefer to use a five- rather than seven-note tuning system, and argue that the tools for smelting and recasting this set of instruments can be found among the materials onstage. A more historically minded group counters that the present set of gongs were fashioned a decade ago as direct replicas of those used during the 1893 Columbian Exposition — the first time such music was heard in this hemisphere — and which now lie in deep storage beneath Chicago's Field Museum. The large gong alone would require multiple castings, the ventilation system couldn't possibly be up to the task, the fumes will kill us all, and according to whose calculation is this a propitious day to begin?

The carpenters are making fine progress on the scaffolding for the ensemble of instruments, and the cadre of elderly folks and children training to be performers have moved on to counting exercises in which they mime the process of grasping the boss and muting the gong before again letting fall the strike of the mallet.

All eyes turn toward the ceiling as it shudders beneath the drop of barbells in the gymnasium overhead. Dead weight thunders, another image of vibration

this time the visible buckling of the ceiling. When the tremor ceases all present meditate on a dozen starry recesses in the firmament. One year ago a torso-sized rosette detached and crashed to the ground, thankfully killing none, and the remaining plaster decorations were promptly culled and carted away.

The potentially calamitous setting into motion of the idiophone.

Tuned metal pongs throughout the space.

The composer has modified the largest gong to his satisfaction and divided among multiple groups the task of tuning the smaller instruments. While sounding the largest gong regularly with his right hand he jots with his left a series of one-page scores for which the page-turner serves as copyist.

The introductory piece, he explains, is the most simple of the bunch. It repeats every sixty-four beats. The largest gong sounds four times within the cycle — one strike for every sixteen beats. We'll play as many cycles as is necessary while the audience finds their seats, makes themselves — ourselves, yourselves — comfortable. Then there will be three other pieces with a varied repertoire of moods, and a louder, more aggressive final piece that unambiguously signals that the program has concluded and it's time to leave. Even as we're listening to a performed piece of music it will be clear that it's time to go. You simply have to trust me that everyone will know what to do when they hear this piece, the one that comes after the final piece in the program. We'll repeat it until the last audience member has left the space. None but the performers will hear its conclusion, a conclusion cast into doubt.

There they sit, cross-legged in a single file, making ready to set out in a newly constructed Norse longship.

The boat's skeleton is inverted, and its spine extends directly above the heads of the seated performers. A gong hangs at each of the ten vertebrae and the structure occupies the center of the room, with the audience closely gathered.

At the front of the line of performers are the twins. The brother takes the prow, with his sister directly behind, close enough that when time permits she can jab him in the kidneys with her mallet. Next are two elderly neighbors in real life who remain skeptical of whether the children are mature enough to participate in the ensemble. They've made their opinions clear. Then come five individuals who didn't wish to be tasked with the design, construction, tuning, or polishing of the instruments and the armature. Finally there's the musician, who sits in the anchor position and is responsible for sounding the largest gong. The composer gives the instruction that they are to play the simple introductory piece for a modest period, but please don't think in minutes and only think in beats insofar as they are relevant to phrases and the whole as meaningfully subdivided by the smaller gongs. Before this can fully sink in, the composer claps out a startling introductory flourish and the ensemble dutifully if sluggishly launches itself into open water. There's a scrape, a bounce of bottoming out, and buoyancy does the rest.

Fisheye distortion warps the inverted musician.

Every fourth four-beat phrase the image is crazed:

smacked with a mallet her image resets to zero time.

Time is beaten into spasmodic respiration, shimmies as it shimmers.

Cataclysmic visual disruption syncs with the ensemble's lowest-pitched and most infrequently produced sound. Whoever polished these instruments did a hell of a job. There's a four-beat phrase and a second, a third, and a fourth, and here comes the red cloth-covered mallet again to punish the reflected image of the musician. The short composition injects itself into the muscle- and sinew-memory of the ensemble, red smothers boss.

Masochism in bronze. This is supposed to hurt.

Every cycle begins and ends with

the largest gong. There is a precise medium-

intensity stroke that produces an exceptionally rich blossom.

The musician pulses in multiples, radiates and dissipates energy. Cyclical and renewable: gray energy. Metal barely has time to settle and once again here comes the clockwork strike.

The larger the gong, the softer its mallet.

The smaller the gong, the more often it's struck.

The one, deaf to its parts.

After five minutes the longship's crew begins to wonder whether the introductory piece has run its course. The performers essay eye contact with the composer, but he's all ears and what he hears is an ensemble just beginning to limber up. He perambulates around the gong structure in a causally ambiguous relationship to the performance. Sometimes his sped-up or slowed-down walk gibes with the pace of the music; sometimes it provides a deliberate, exaggerated counterpoint; and there are periods where his walking suggests an impoverished form of conducting. He cocks his head, nearly laying it on his own upraised shoulder, and with cupped hands alternates covering and uncovering one ear and then the other. From time to time the flapping of his cupped hands accelerates into a uniquely experienced tremolo.

Boredom or acoustics or choreography.

Red floods boss

smothers nipple; the anchor

gets knocked for a loop.

Four thousand and ninety-six beats later

her reflection is clobbered for the sixty-fourth time. She tries to look away, does her best to keep from even momentarily locking eyes with her tired, sweaty, repetition-dazed self because the next thing you know red swings low, executes energy transfer, sets the scene

athrob.

When driving through the park on a bright summer day try to avoid the temptation to study the sky and undersides of clouds and tree branches reflected in the hood of a newly waxed car.

When tending the largest gong avoid becoming hypnotized.

The performers have been counseled not to think in measures or minutes, but we must be approaching the twenty-minute mark in a piece created to soundtrack the search for seats. Eyes are trained on the composer. Sensing the slight elevation of temperature caused by the collective stare, he responds with a right-hand thumbs-up and with his left the counterclockwise roll of an index finger that signifies continue. The page-turner bends down and offers an ear for a whispered communiqué; he quickly straightens and with hand gestures identical to those of the composer mouths the words SOUNDS GREAT!

At the one-hour mark a shared thought dawns on the performers: what if this has to end?

They're not ready to dispose so quickly of this musical material. It has long since assumed an otherworldly courtly cast, and the performers bask in the pride of getting it right.

Apt cycles of vowels alone.

All mourn in advance the passing of what had previously seemed impossibly simple and overlong. The composer and performers are in wordless agreement: there can be no rash decision to draw to a close this slow and ever more steady onrush of sound. As the piece spills into its second hour, it begins to click for a group of teenagers who had previously been the most dismissive and uninvolved of audience members. They push to the front of the crowd, clustering in a semi-circle behind the largest gong. The teens focus intently on the gong's nipple, and with every strike they coo and laugh and moan as the mallet obliterates their inverted portrait.

Splashes in bronze.

The teens improvise a technique for rapidly clapping polyrhythms, a curious, stylized gesture akin to washing one's hands. Their clapping subdivides the cycle into more uneven, more kinetic proportions. The musician, forever stationed at the largest gong, responds by dragging down the pulse so that the clapping group is able to double their tempo and upshift to a next level of adrenalized density.

Ninety minutes into this introductory piece the composer decides that they have reached a point where performer substitutions begin to be necessary. Composer and page-turner deliver taps to the twins' shoulders to signal that they should prepare to switch out, that their replacements are ready. When the twins finally surrender their spots, they topple to their left and sink into exhausted sleep. The substitutions are accomplished without interruption.

The replacement performers arrive with a novel instruction from the composer: when they feel that they are ready to do so, they are welcome to deviate from the written part.

At first neither replacement finds the confidence that the time has arrived.

The elderly neighbors are the next to be replaced, and so it goes down the line.

The ensemble of clapping teens similarly cycles through performers, and with new blood it provides reenergized and often perilously loose rhythmic articulation.

The introductory composition evolves through the eventual rhythmic displacement of each of its pitches, the bedrock exception being that of the largest gong. The musician would never agree to a substitution — not that there was ever a tap on her shoulder.

Anchor solo

for fixed rudder

for faithful accompanist inverted

displaced by rests

by still-longer silences, unforeseen

linings-up in time, by the simultaneous attack of five, six, or more gongs and the ripple of a broken metal chord sweeping down the ship's spine. Randomized soundings of vertebrae. The turnover of performers accelerates to where each individual taking up a mallet delivers two or three well-considered strikes, then bails.

After several dozen participants have cycled through the clapping ensemble, the group fades to silence. This transition provides the opportunity for the composer and page-turner to indulge in one last scavenge in the junk heap.

The composer fashions a small battery of molar-sized percussion instruments attached to a curve of bone that resembles the jaw of a large animal. The page-turner soberly pings and bends and bows a rusty saw.

Nine gongs hang abandoned.

To collide repeatedly, crabwise transform, to alter orbits

until composer's and page-turner's actions morph into the sweep-

ing of trash and the musician's reflected self hovers at a halt.

From the silence of deepest center where

the crack of the bat doesn't arrive

all waves crash at once.

As the full measure of applause begins to sound

as waves succumb to gravity and sleeper and insomniac alike unburden; as a squadron of cymbal crashes reverses; as stomps, ridiculous hoots, and ricochets of joyous hollering fill the space

rejigger, transduce, awaken the ear.

The composer and page-turner deflect applause, turn toward and clap for the musician, who rises with eyes shut and displays her back to the audience.

The musician imagines that each performance will end in mishap.

She expects each performance to proceed by way of mishap and to end with telltale overlong silence. With the wrong silence, with an embarrassed gap, with a perfunctory and polite response, with merely polite conversation, and with post-concert reciprocal avoidance. She rues the fact that she's perfectly sober and is of mixed feelings that in a few minutes she'll be drinking as fast as she can. Impossible not to overshoot one's mark one's question mark.

The musician reaches into a front pocket and clicks her phone alive as the door at the back of the stage swings open and six arms wave to her. The folks who had been listening from the other side of the wall greet her warmly. Instant disorientation: are these the same people who facilitated the load-in, the soundcheck, the family-style dinner, and the pre-concert contact high? Don't let them see you sense you've never laid eyes.

Who ages so visibly over the course of a single performance?

Time moves we don't know how outside this calibration.

The shower of applause abates, resumes.

Ushered into a dark passageway, the musician finds herself embracing these three strangers, the overnight staff, one after the next, so many cares surrendered in glancing, meaningful bodily contact and the sparing of unnecessary words. The staff gestures toward the far end of the passage: the door to the dressing room. Not that any of this looks remotely familiar from the perspective of the stage at one's back. Reset for the counting down, for the stage in one's sails.

Disengage airlock. The musician finds herself alone, is grateful to be in an incongruous nether-space and especially in the dark, listening to applause, listening to proof of a performance now past, ready to listen through the dying and disappearance of the smallest sound.

The musician wonders if she should return or just keep walking.

Flee the building, drink elsewhere, come back an hour from now?

Should she let a year go by? Is the more responsible course of action never to return to this town? For whom is her absence an issue if she never again touches down in this country?

She opens the door at the end of the hall and finds in lieu of the antici-
pated chest-high row of mirrors an altogether different space:

a soaring ceiling, a wall of windows opposite with mid-morning light
burning through and opening onto field and then, distantly, forest. An
immediate apprehension of echoing surfaces, and a stone floor cool
to the touch even through the sole of one's shoe. The twice-muffled
dapple of distant applause blends with the aural sheen of this enor-
mous, depopulated room.

Clapping and hollering hails from a scarcely recalled world.

An audience awaits, but that was

when and daylight is

w o w

Why reverse course? Why set foot in that darkened sphere when we should be gathering here?

The theoretically infinite number of instruments and dimmed lights in the fateful cabin be damned. Here we have at the exact center of this immense foyer — a space we all must have passed through prior to the evening's performance — in this ideal

equinoctial environment

a grand piano

the patience of a grand piano

parked and unattended

As the musician moves toward the instrument waiting at the center of the room, the double doors through which she entered swing open and applause shoots forth unmuted, momentarily stakes its claim on her — a brief heterophonous din — and then the doors swing shut. She wheels around and makes eye contact with those sheepish first audience members to attempt an escape prior to the encore. The musician takes an immediate liking to them, startles by blowing a kiss.

She has an idea. People will exhaust themselves clamoring for an encore, pack up and leave, and on their way out they'll discover her seated at the piano, playing. An encore already begun.

Those who would prefer not to suffer through the encore will be the ones who first encounter it, but they're free to keep right on walking.

She reflects that someone did her the service of designing and building this instrument.

A few scattered chords demonstrate that the tuning is better than anticipated. The audience will soon be exiting en masse the performance of isolation, absorption, breath, all-of-a-mind focus.

Here I am seated at the piano, looking so grand.

Here I am, without a care in the world, seated at the piano and just waiting for the big reveal. I would happily wait forever.

This is my instrument. I know where it ends. It will always be my first instrument, and for a time I thought of it as my one instrument and also as the means of visualizing music. Then I dove into the spaces between keys and learned what's not piano. The piano is neither cello nor bloodcurdling shriek. It includes neither pitch wheel nor portamento ribbon. It's not the sonification of data. I know the piano as touch, I turn to the piano as a machine to amplify touch, a machine to flesh out touch; it presses flesh with, it shakes hands with the machinery of my arms, hands, and fingertips. To the extent that I am free to be ignorant of what I do it is because of my fingertips.

The child in my fingertips.

Two more couples venture through the double doors. The musician acknowledges their presence by serving up four unique soundings, each a spontaneous portrait, four brief epithets like so:

third-to-lowest note on the piano, sudden and grave in its appearance; two fragrant mid-keyboard clusters, at first blush difficult to distinguish from one another, but with the second a more profound dissonance hovers as reconsideration; and finally a clear, widely-voiced splash of a chord that bespeaks kinship, favoritism, attraction. More and more people enter the foyer, stumble upon the musician's renewed intimacy with this instrument.

I can't believe the serene good fortune of choosing the wrong door and again the piano chooses me. Welcomes me back. I know, my fingertips know, the bottoms of my feet know that this contact with the piano marks a clean break from what came before. This many years later whatever I choose to do, however I orient myself, however I commit myself, whatever I make of this opportunity will be the better for time spent away, will differ in kind because of the fallow period, whether or not true love waits at very least I manifest the reward of inaction.

Not long after the appearance of those first few individuals fleeing the performance space and finding themselves amid the unplanned encore—embarrassed, hide-your-eyes non-acknowledgement of the musician—the applause finally dies away. Back in the darkened sphere those folks most desiring of an encore, whatever form that might take, give up and grab their coats, drain their drinks, offer handshakes and hugs, and blearily and reluctantly make for the exit while debating the evening's unscroll, finding themselves

bot-

tle-necked then ambushed by revenant pianist. Each audience member crossing the threshold into the bright foyer triggers one in a series of pointillistic attacks, small releases of energy summoned as if by tripwire.

The musician's eyes admit nothing but keyboard. She senses the ebb and the flatlining of a final small wave of applause, but does not fully register the audience having silently massed around the piano. She's unwilling to look.

The aperiodic to-ings and fro-ings of the double doors and subsequent fugitive whispers indicate to her the emptying out of the performance space.

The inversion of the hourglass from enforced perpetual dusk.

Gravity's pull

terminates in the keyboard

in rising hammers and lightly pummeled strings. It terminates for now in an intuitive fingertipped scheme. A steady state of volume obtains for each attack, whether businesslike or declarative single notes, increasingly softer voices within progressively larger chords, open-palm and forearm clusters sketching pillows or clouds, and the gentlest double forearm bump, just for show, in which hammers leap toward strings but hang suspended shy of their mark.

Sunlight on my cheek. Sunlight on my ear and neck and right arm. Slight imbalance of warmth issuing from the wall of windows. Sunlight says lift up your eyes

but I'm not there yet. The keyboard determines my field of vision. I'm still measuring the fingered distances of intervals, easing into wider voicings, testing the equidistance among three black keys against the side of my hand. Trying to think x number of steps ahead so as to shade into not thinking. It's all part of learning to play the piano. Attack velocity and sustain, the practice of listening within a sound, to anticipate decay, to model decay. To replicate. Repetition is elsewhere and meditating on it seems in no way productive. This is not how I care to acknowledge the sunlight and so I stop.

I raise my head to confront the scythe of humans.

A grinning and expectant mass, and the negligible breeze chills.

All I wanted as a pianist was to clear

my head, so here I sit.

I've imagined returning to the piano in precisely this manner.

Clamber onto the raft of the piano, the envoi that is the instrument, adieu. Years ago I stopped playing the better to start again. Moments ago I did the same. What you just heard was reacquaintance, preliminary measurements, fitting fingers to keys. A preamble of figurative stabs and salutations.

Greetings, you found me.

A crescent archipelago of eyes ringing 'round

all eyes on the dreamer, to cast off

in retrospect, shipwrect

Now I'm prepared—

A dream, age twelve, of improvising, before the word meant any-thing to me. I dreamed its signification. I saw myself playing without reference to anything I previously had learned, I moved in a space of non-anticipation, calm compelled, and when I picked up the guitar— an unfamiliar instrument—I was just as curious as anyone else what might come next. I listened to my own playing. I floated separate, I haunted. In the dream my playing was the subject of acclaim. It be-came a daytime-television phenomenon. This girl simply picks up an instrument and out comes a beguilingly moody music that never re-peats, and she's twelve years old. Just imagine where, given time, this might go. Toward the end of the dream I found myself searching for the instrument that I thought I had left leaning against a wall, behind a door.

Evidently I'm still emptying out.

A further spell passes. The archipelago of audience starts to shift, hints at anticipation and impatience through small eddies of colliding shoulders.

I find myself wondering how long I must wait to play this instrument anew. Not to receive the instrument as recombinant form, as vectored form. What does it mean to reshuffle the deck? The instrument at which I am seated impresses me as sufficiently solid, sufficiently reliable that I could excuse myself and return twenty years from now to pick up the thread of events. This piano is not going to collapse, to scatter, to elude precise reconstruction. There's a temptation to lower the lid and climb aboard, to seek out the most comfortable position in which to wait. For now I should take the opportunity to focus on my seated self, beginning with the problematic lower back, to try to better understand my posture. Make overdue corrections. To discover that uniquely imprinted tempo — the tempo of this very morning — at which one breath might evenly follow the next. I can discover that tempo in order to set it aside. I can let flesh and physical process dominate the sensory apparatus such that I don't trouble myself with preparation, but engage gravity:

let fall   let rise   make fall

I can't abide gravity. Can't trust myself.

I should have continued to wait, should have better understood the breathing self, better forgotten the breathing body, forgotten the piano. I should have foregone any precise notion of improvisation. Instead my hands surrender to gravity and fall into an opening move I'll describe as an eight-fingered gambit of three dissonantly offset versions of the same chord dumped from a passing car. My brain jostles awake and I find myself assessing options for a next move. Don't follow a first with a second — find another first one. I don't know which direction I'm headed, but the fact of the piano tells me I need a plan, and that's not how I'd hoped to begin.

I slam out the same chord a second time.

Which is not another first time. Let it die.

When the repeated chord is fully extinguished, I remove my hands from the keyboard and place them at my side. I try not to recall anything resembling musical content. I eschew anecdote, try not to picture my hands. I scoot the piano bench closer, rededicate myself to the task, and the feral screech of the bench against the stone floor is satisfying enough that I instinctively try to replicate it.

Thankfully I fail. I produce the most demure of scrapes, and in doing so smack my left hand's knuckles against the lower edge of the piano. In an entirely overeager fashion I do it again, to punish myself, and punish myself musically. This time I'm able to repeat the gesture with more success, if that's how to describe two knocks on the least resonant spot on a piano.

A deep breath, and a marginally simplified sketch of the initial chord.

I'm hazarding a real-time analysis by subtracting notes, seeing what remains, with no particular logic apart from that of diminishment, of contraction, of rejecting the unearned pleasure of hands spread the way hands like it.

Instead of playing the truncated chord a second time, I attempt to block my internal debate with a right-forearm attack that cuts hard to silence. What's the point of this sequence of arbitrary leaps, each of which disappears down the rabbit hole? Left-forearm smash, three harmonics sounded on the strings of the piano's lowest octave. Et cetera.

I once again halt, so far from

emptied, marveling that I had thought

myself free to approach the instrument anew.

This is crippling, this tide-turning encroach of reproach. I never should have sat down at this piano, not even as an excuse to pass the time. I want to disassemble the thing, torch the strings, strip the screws, splinter the soundboard, liberate the fallboard, saw off its legs, hula-hoop the harp, turn the instrument into one more heap of destroyed parts, and casually sweep it where no one will ever think to look beneath some nonexistent rug.

Now then! Now that the audience

I offer up my winningest grin.

They're happy to reciprocate.

They're waiting for that hard-won encore to begin in earnest.

I haven't yet burned through the entirety of amassed good will. We're still in this together, and I'm ringed by a group of souls eager to experience — as just moments ago I had been eager to proffer — the piano as the obverse of our overnight flight. Sunday morning slumming gown. This is an unreal encounter, doused by daylight.

All present and assembled most likely assume that after two false starts I'm recomposing myself, and that this most spontaneous of encores happens now.

The problem is that I find myself seated at a piano

and don't have the faintest idea how to begin. Nor have I any impulse to do so. With each passing second it's increasingly unlikely that I'll start again, that I'll make the mistake of once again touching the keys. I sense I've begun another indefinite hiatus, and my smile curls upward in the direction of outright laughter.

A quick glance reveals faces of judgment withheld trending in the direction of genuine concern. I suddenly leap into a standing position and cut loose with the wildest of self-lacerating cackles.

No one takes the invitation. There go your theories of laughter as reactionary corrective, as eccentricity put on notice, behavior to be sanded down. As a last resort I throw my hands skyward.

The surrender is not accepted.

A full minute of sunshot silence.

Failure dawns and it breaks over the crowd that that's all there is, my huckleberry friends. There's a small amount of scattered clapter, disbelief, confusion, dispersal, discussion, and ostrichlike persistence of wait-and-see. I picture my face as the freeze frame of a wave crashing. With hands still above my head I signal with the smallest flutter of fingertips. Incomplete rictus permits me to tiptoe, and I make my way back across the foyer, toward the double doors to resume my search for the dressing room.

I manage a strangled good night smilingly corrected as good morning.

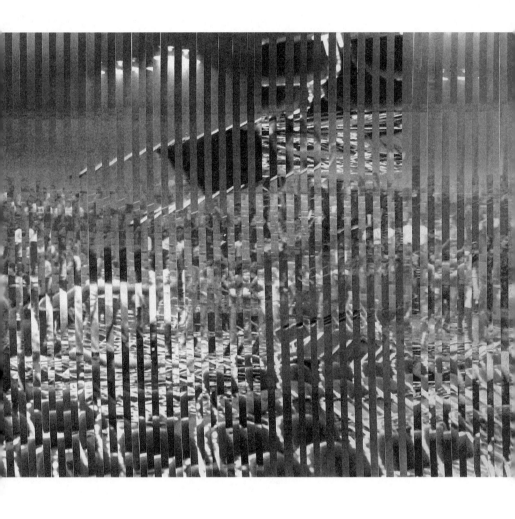

Afterword

In the fall of 2013 I enjoyed finishing *Records Ruin the Landscape: John Cage, the Sixties, and Sound Recording* so much that I thought I might like to finish another book. I was ready to continue writing about music, but in this case, and unlike *Records Ruin the Landscape*, I was inclined to do so without reference to sound recording, networks of distribution, technologies of representation, or the comparative study of listening cultures. I thought to set aside the textures of the time stamps of recordings. I was also ready to write a long poem.

The musical situation that I found myself eager to describe is a concert of experimental or improvised music. I realize that doesn't tell you much. But this initially baggy subject proved self-generating; it became the opportunity to write about solo performance, free improvisation, text scores, instrument building, time killing, masochism, performer psychology, audience behavior, audience and performer bad behavior, the all-night concert, sleeping through a concert, waking up in the midst of a concert, the deskilling and reskilling of conventionally trained musicians, the curious and occasionally vestigial role of the composer in experimental music, a lifetime of fraught relations with one's first instrument, and more.

Orienting my thoughts toward live performance and a kind of musical activity that explicitly frames itself as improvised, I found myself reflecting on the process of doing things once and once only.

For a number of decades—since I was a teenager in the early 1980s—those impulses that otherwise would have been realized as poems for me found their form as song lyrics. As far as I can recall I have never written a poem—only songs. In spite of private aims and admonishments (the song lyric must work as well on the page as it does when performed, etc.) these lyrics remained miniatures. They have also been constrained by the strange fate that they will be sung. Thus I had planned for some time to disburden myself of a long poem, one that unlike a song would be undertaken without an end in sight. Whenever this internal broken record starts to play, I recall Laura (Riding) Jackson's *Twenty Poems Less* (1930). It might be my favorite title of any book. This title provided the impetus for the group Gastr del Sol's EP "20 Songs Less" (1994), and more than twenty years later I'm still mulling it over, specifically what it suggests about artistic production as a form of counting down—sometimes tossing sandbags out of the hot-air balloon, sometimes just moving toward zero.

I committed to one poem, and one poem less.

It's easy not to write about music. I was compelled to write a long description of a fictional musical performance given the way that live performance is meaningfully elided in works such as John Ashbery's "The Concert" (from *Three Poems*), which is largely preamble to a concert that suddenly has already taken place, and Kazuo Ishiguro's *The Unconsoled*, which is structured around a concert that never comes to pass. The double duty of a long poem that is also an experiment in music writing came to seem less rarefied when reflecting on the examples of Alexander Kluge and Nathaniel Mackey, in whose work literature becomes the site of exemplary writing about, respectively, media history and jazz and improvised music.

The first public airing of the poem as a work in progress was a performance in January 2014, in which my reading was electronically manipulated by C. Spencer Yeh and accompanied by percussionist Eli Keszler. The word "accompanied" doesn't do justice to a style of playing that was every bit as autonomous as the reading — it was accompaniment in the sense of occupying the same time and space. (After this first performance, Tony Conrad reported that he had to restrain himself from invading the stage and acting out the role of the page-turner.) At the MIT List Visual Arts Center in the fall of 2014, as part of the exhibition *Open Tunings*, the piece was revisited and expanded as a collaborative installation and performance with Eli Keszler under the title *One and One Less*. *Open Tunings* was conceived by curator Henriette Huldisch as a sequential, three-part group exhibition, in which an artist was invited to present a performance in one of the List's galleries, and then to have the "residue" — Huldisch's term — of the performance remain on display for the following month. Eli's and my installation consisted of four large wall drawings that I made based on the poem, as well as a sound installation that Eli designed with seven large wall-mounted boxes, each containing more than a dozen transducers with which to produce a battery of small percussive attacks (wood, metal, plastic, and long strings) when activated by a cut-up, multichannel recording of myself reading the first thirty minutes of the poem. The fronts of the boxes were covered with white panels so that none of their appealingly mechanized guts were displayed. To open the exhibition, Eli and I performed in the gallery while accompanied by the visually spare but sonically clangorous installation. Audio documentation of the installation as well as a studio recording of a subsequent duo performance appeared in 2017 as *One and One Less*, the inaugural LP release of Ugly Duckling Presse Records (UDPR).

An art historian friend once told me how much he enjoyed that charmed, neither/nor stretch of time between turning in a book manuscript and its actual publication. The work's finished, but it hasn't really begun to age; the book has its whole life ahead of it. With *Records Ruin the Landscape* what I liked best was taking it on the road and making what I could of the book as a set of arguments to be considered through readings, public discussions, and live music performances. Prior to its completion as a book, *Now that the audience is assembled* has already taken the form of wall drawings, sound recordings, a sound installation, and live performances. I look forward to those realizations — each one, one fewer — it might assume in the future.

Acknowledgments

My first debt (debth) of gratitude for most anything having to do with poetry goes to Susan Howe. I was an enthusiastic reader of Susan's for years before we began working together in 2004. Even though I focused on poetry in graduate school, I'll confess that my attention drifted elsewhere — multiple elsewheres — until Susan and I began creating collaborative performance works based on her writing. In my experience, I'd be hard-pressed to identify a more gratifying collaboration or a more meaningful education with regard to literature. One of the things that Susan and I have in common is a fascination with the unending interplay between graphic mark and sounding. This check and balance, check and productive imbalance between written and sounded poem has been the primary technique for creating *Now that the audience is assembled*. How could the sounded and the written balance one another? Impossible idea.

I am grateful to Ben Lerner, who challenged me to write a book of poetry around the time that he started to switch it up to craft marvels in fiction. Ben was this book's first reader, and a superb one. When I told him early on that one conceit of the poem was that it was to be a first poem, he eerily beat me to my own punch line: "And last poem?" My next readers (and then I'll stop calling them out one by one) were Cathy Bowman, John Corbett, Terri Kapsalis, and Amnon Wolman, each of whom has contributed decades of feedback to all manner of projects in music, writing, and otherwise, and all of whom helped me to better recognize and build upon commonalities between this book and *Records Ruin the Landscape*.

The musician, composer, and visual artist Eli Keszler has been crucial in bringing this text to bear upon live performances, its realization as an LP, and our collaborative exhibition at the MIT List Visual Arts Center that was curated by Henriette Huldisch. Thanks go to the List for their willingness to allow the reproduction of an installation photograph, and especially to Mark Linga, who facilitated the permission. Mónica de la Torre, Clinton Krute, and others at *BOMB* made possible the first performance of this material by a trio of myself, Eli, and C. Spencer Yeh. The *One and One Less* LP (and its beautifully designed poster, which includes an excerpt from an earlier version of this poem) was released by Ugly Duckling Presse Records (UDPR), the brainchild and sweatchild of Matvei Yankelevitch and Michael Barron.

Thank you, John Sparagana, for creating the cover artwork and a host of related collages.

I appreciate the stellar, ever-creative efforts of Ken Wissoker and the folks with whom I've had the pleasure to work at Duke University Press: Amy Ruth Buchanan, Diane Grossé, Sara Leone, Michael McCullough, Olivia Polk, Laura Sell, and Julie Thomson. Thanks are also due to Julie Agoos, Tim Barnes, Caroline Bergvall, Roger Bowman, Ruth Bowman, Jeff Clark, Corbett vs. Dempsey, Lawrence English, Barbara Epler, Ann Faurest, Matthew Goulish, Andy Graydon, Bill Grubbs, Susan Grubbs, Lin Hixson, Devin Johnston, Branden W. Joseph, Lawrence Kumpf, Pierre-Yves Macé, Les presses du réel, Sho Sugita, Taku Sugimoto, Ellen Tremper, Taku Unami, Yu Wakao, Hamza Walker, Marjorie Welish, Red Wierenga, Kyoko Yabusaki, and Jeffrey Yang, with especial gratitude to Cathy Bowman and Emmett Bowman-Grubbs.

Finally, I would like to acknowledge my departed and much-missed friends Tony Conrad and Luc Ferrari, whose art and ideas infuse this book.

Image Credits